About the Author

After seven years of traversing the world of music journalism, Jess Conkwright has found a desire to tell ethereal stories about the complexities of women and their journeys. She has written and produced two short films, works as a creative editor and enjoys writing children's stories. She is obsessed with cult culture, historical fiction and anything to do with time travel. Jess lives in Los Angeles.

A Person, Abbreviated

Jess Conkwright

A Person, Abbreviated

Olympia Publishers
London

www.olympiapublishers.com
OLYMPIA PAPERBACK EDITION

A CIP catalogue record for this title is
available from the British Library.

ISBN: 978-1-80439-896-8

This is a work of fiction.
Names, characters, places and incidents originate from the writer's
imagination. Any resemblance to actual persons, living or dead, is
purely coincidental.

First Published in 2024

Olympia Publishers
Tallis House
2 Tallis Street
London
EC4Y 0AB

Printed in Great Britain

To all the ones who took me in when I was searching.

Moments with people sometime, somewhere.

Aaron wore multi-colored scarves and he was as impossible as he was brilliant, a savant, a St. Vincent. He raved about how handsome his boyfriend was and wanted me to be at their wedding whenever that happened. He was friendly but angry, spoke of Paris as if he would be buried there. I told him I would visit Montpellier and toast to him, even if he were dead by the time I arrived.

We made coffee together in the kitchen in Positano. He restored antique furniture and cried when I sang him a song I wrote. He had the saddest eyes I had ever seen and he played the guitar better than my mother told stories. He spoke Italian, I spoke English and we understood each other perfectly. Once I thought he asked me to eat an elephant with him, and at that moment I was so happy I might have.

She told me as she sipped her Pinot Noir she had a garden on her roof and she was glad she left California. While in high school in LA she had a boyfriend with a gambling problem. She could never say his name aloud so she called him "The man who fell from grace." This man taught her things no high school girl should ever be taught, tilting and poker and pawning her off to his friends for kicks. She was his loyal spaniel and she loved him like a wanderer of the open road, craving the notion that the next adventure would be the one that saved them. Emulating a humiliating version of Bonnie and Clyde, they would eat Taco Bell in the back of her beige Lexus and fuck until he went back into the casino to lose all his money and hers. When he was away, she read Dostoyevsky and smoked Gauloises and promised herself one day she would move to New York and write naked in her living room. I knew she made her living as a writer, but I never asked if she did it naked.

We read Kafka and Hemingway while we made dollar store spaghetti in the dark. I thought it was romantic, but really he had no electricity in that little cabin with the corners stacked with books. We were fifteen miles outside of town. He dropped me off at my dorm as daylight peaked through the blackness. Before I got out of the car he handed me a Death Cab for Cutie CD and told me it was a letter from God. I played it over and over in my room and never wanted to wash my hair, for it smelled like firewood from the relic he inhabited. He had no luxuries and I was his virgin Mona Lisa. To me… it was a life. The next day I watched him as he stood in front of the class, analyzing Radiohead videos and talking about Prague. I decided I would do my dissertation on multiple personality disorders in criminals. He gave me an A and told me that I was so much more than what I thought I was.

He looked like a soccer player on his day off, with perfectly peppered hair and dimples that made me weak. I knew he was trouble and I didn't care. When I got off the train I told him I needed toothpaste. When we were in the aisle at Whole Foods I said something I believed was rather clever. He tried to kiss me then, and I stopped him and explained something about not being that kind of girl. I was clutching a bundle of rosemary and I wondered how much more potent the smell would be if it were smashed between our two naked bodies. I checked out without so much as a glance at him, feeling his obvious discomfort and tension at my rejection. We spent many days together. He thought it was strange I never drank wine, but he told me at the end that I inspired him as he put the back of his hand on my cheek. When I left him he wrote me a letter, and it would be four years before I would talk to him again. I asked him why he ignored me upon my return to the states, and he told me it was the right thing to do.

I sat on the edge of her bed as she talked about shiny curtains with rugs that matched. "Do you like them? They're shiny. They're so shiny, and I also bought these wine glasses for half off. We could have a party! Let's have a party!" She was wearing a green t-shirt that read *Kiss me, I'm Irish.* She had wild caramel curls. I wondered if she ever cut them, they seemed so untouched. The cocaine was visible on her nose, but I didn't comment on it. I loved the way her house smelled, like she did nothing but bake pies and cookies all day. She offered me a line and I took it not because I wanted to, but because I was annoyed at the cadence of her voice. It was good, and I wanted more, but then decided to text my best friend instead and get the hell out of there. I asked the curtain girl for a couple of lines to take with me, promising I would pay her back with vodka later. She complied, and as I was leaving she started doing the dishes and singing along to Janis Joplin. I yelled goodbye to her but she didn't hear me.

"I'm Daisy," she told me as our group walked closer to the water to hear the last band. The air smelled like saltwater and beer, and I breathed it in heartily. It was just chilly enough for me to covet Daisy's faux fur orange jacket. The crowds of people around us migrated rather quietly in the same direction, and it felt like a soft hug when it often felt like suffocation. Daisy's eyes were watery and her skin was caked with emerald glitter. She told me her boyfriend left her for a girl with the same name, and I thought how odd it was that there were two Daisy's in Barcelona. I also wondered if the other one was as pretty as she. Daisy held my hand all through M83's set, and I told her that their latest album changed my life. "Seeing them is like seeing God." Before she went home she gave me a purple butterfly barrette and said I wasn't like most Americans.

"Eggs are good for you," he said. "My nephews eat eggs and bacon every morning." I rolled my eyes. "I can't imagine that's good, all those hormones…" He scoffed. "Eat your scone." It was busy at our regular brunch place, where we had our regular spot at the bar and the bartender insisted on keeping us up to date on her new artwork. Later, he showed me his old black and white headshots from the nineties. He told me he was glad he quit acting. I noticed he was grayer but with the same cheeky smile.

She buried her mother in the cemetery on the southern side of the Ohio River, right next to a post office that had been closed for years.

I held her hand as the pastor spoke of love and Christ and heaven.

She did not cry.

Afterwards, we got tea at the bar we both worked at in college.

We wore short skirts back then and told lies to the managers about why we were going out back to the alley.

The bar had a different name.

The once very lively speakeasy was now pristine and commercial.

We found no remnants of our past.

She looked at me and asked "Do you remember Ayla?"

I nodded and said I remembered her fondly. A beautiful solemn girl, who cussed and had her wits about her.

She told me she thought Ayla killed herself in a Texas jail. I shook my head and said it was probably just a rumor. She looked pensive for a moment.

She ordered a bourbon. I did the same.

She said her mother's grave should have read "puppet master". But she couldn't figure out if it were her or God who finally cut her strings.

We drove higher and higher into the canyon as we talked about the murders. He pulled over on the gravel road next to a driveway and we got out to head towards the mansion where it all happened. He turned around quickly, making a scuffle with his sneakers and it made me gasp. The world around us was hushed and still. I asked him, "Would you protect me from the hippies?" His hazel eyes burned into me, even in the darkness. He ran his fingers through his sandy brown hair and replied, "I would kill that guard shack guy for you." I looked towards his gaze and saw an old man in his seventies sitting in a booth reading a paper. I shook my head and giggled as he pulled out a pack of Marlborough's. "I didn't know you smoked," I said. He grabbed my hand and whispered in my ear, "I never light it."

Her name was Rio (or so she claimed), and I was dubious of her from the start. She did sketch comedy and had a birthmark on her arm the size of a grapefruit. We were supposed to be quiet the last hour of the meeting, but she never was. She would always find some newbie to whisper excitedly to while the rest of us tinkered away on our laptops. Her mere presence was incredibly daunting but as weeks went by, I realized she was a lonely girl who probably didn't have many friends to talk to outside of our coven. She often wore the same red plaid pants and her chest moved up and down when she laughed. She boasted about her Elvis musical every week but I never got to read it. Maybe the newbies needed her somehow, and I eventually made peace with that.

"Are you doing drugs tonight, young lady?" a beautiful girl called to me as I changed into the tube top she let me borrow.

My clothes were too 'classy' for where we were going.

My mother's friend brought me to this place.

I suddenly felt free in a way I had never been before.

The beautiful girl's bare feet were hanging outside of the mini cooper that we parked in the warehouse lot.

The club was all ages, so we got right in.

I sprayed Charlie White perfume in my hair as we frolicked down the dark hallway.

"I don't think it's kicking in." I said after a few moments, leaning against the bathroom stall.

She had the biggest blue eyes I had ever seen and I wanted to drown in them.

She stuck the key under my nose again.

I called her my soulmate. She giggled and said "I'm Marie and I'll be whatever you want me to be."

She floated with me towards the music again.

She told me she wanted to make out with someone and was ok if it was a girl.

I gave her a lollipop and kissed her. Her lips were softer and gentler than a boy's.

She showed me how to dance like a bunny.

My legs were very heavy.

The music got louder and I could feel the bass in my skull and in my breasts.

She grabbed me by the shoulders.

"Here, take my bracelets. I have to go for a while and no one outside can see these."

She put them all the way up my arm and it gave me goosebumps, even though I was sweating.

The beads looked like candy but I knew I couldn't eat them.

Everyone around me said the word "*Plur*."

My mother's friend said it was time to go, and I was glad I wasn't high anymore. I never saw Marie again and my father threw out all her bracelets.

"I have so many things to read at home, why do I need to check out more books?" he asked me as we walked into the library. He was growing out his beard because his show just got canceled. "You wanted to come here," I said and he nodded. We walked up and down the aisles as he talked about how disorganized his life was. He told me he didn't know who his real friends were anymore because everything changed when he became famous. He put his hand on the small of my back and said he knew I would always be real with him. He asked me if I could help him with his long and arduous stint in celibacy. I laughed. "You're like my brother. If anything were going to happen it would have happened years ago." He stopped, holding a book out in front of his chest. I could smell the pages, that smell so familiar, the mustiness, the spit and dirty fingers. I immediately regretted saying it. He set the book down in a place where it didn't belong and took long glides to the double doors. I trailed behind him, a little embarrassed and a little mad at myself. Once we were outside, he put on his glasses and pulled his hat down towards his eyes. As I stood next to him, he put his arm around my shoulder and said "Let's go somewhere quiet."

"Do you know how I send him messages? By blowing him off."

I nodded, understanding most of what she was saying.

Her silver hair illuminated her face and I wanted to reach for her hand across the table, but that's not what you do when someone is your boss. At least a boss like this one.

A tear dropped from her cheek into her untouched spaghetti.

She took a long deep inhale and waved the waiter over, giving the universal sign for the check. She didn't ask for a doggie bag and I never got used to her nonchalant wasting of food. She didn't have her nap today, and I wondered if she remembered we had a meeting at the studio in the morning. After a bad day she would hide away in her bed as I would be frantically making calls upstairs, covering up her inability to function. I wanted to quit the job, but I had bills to pay. I also greatly admired her philanthropy and her past diligence to her company. She wasn't who she once was, and I often wondered how many people she would have at her funeral.

As we drove past my local wine bar, I told him from the passenger seat that I went there weekly for wine and impromptu poetry sessions with the regulars. He told me he lost the rights to frequent there in a breakup. "You should come back, Silverlake misses you," I said. He glanced at me before rolling through a corner stop sign, making the car to the left of us slam on his breaks. "But it doesn't miss your driving." He laughed and slapped the front of my thigh, and I thought how easy it could be, to just allow this cool guy to be my boyfriend and peel away the accumulated cobwebs from my date book.

One night she told me she hated her sister.

"You will never understand what that's like," she said. And I knew I wouldn't.

Her hair was too dark. And her skin was too fair.

When she drank she would always get angry at someone.

Sweet during the rising sun, exhausting when the moon showed its face.

She was talented but by the end of it I didn't care.

Her apartment smelled like oranges and she used chapstick incessantly. She once said Kurt Cobain taught her everything she knew.

We lived together with our best friends.

As I watched him play the drums, his mother handed me a bottle of water "It'll mean more to him if you bring it, dear."

I took it onstage and placed it by his feet.

He gave me a wink and I could barely breathe.

Later he would bring me water after the four of us partied.

After we danced and laughed and promised it would always be this way, he placed the glass by my bed and kissed my hair.

And sometimes I wanted him to touch me.

Maybe he wanted to wait until the time was perfect. But then it was too late.

He moved out.

And we moved on.

She held flippers in her hand and I noticed her before she noticed me. As my bare feet grazed the sand, I felt the night wind on my shoulders and smiled in the darkness. The ocean always feels better at night. The woman walking towards me was naked and dripping with salty water, her long black hair draped and glistening over her breasts. We walked close enough together that our shoulders could have touched, and I wanted them to…I wanted her to electrify me with some of her magic. She smelled of gardenias and palo santo and when she said hello I watched her lips move in slow motion. After she and I passed each other we both looked back for a moment before we disappeared in our own dimension with the fog.

She listened to R.E.M. with the car windows down.

When I was four I asked her what religion meant.

She said that God and Man were one in the same.

She told me that each lived in the other.

"So, I'm God?" I asked her.

I felt the breeze whip through my dirty blonde hair as she laughed.

Her wide crimson-colored mouth seemed to only smile and tell truths.

When I was seven her crystal ocean eyes gleamed as she described her out of body experiences.

She floated around the house and heard demons in the kitchen.

We ate chocolate at midnight and she would listen to me read. She took me on hikes in autumn, and I loved watching the leaves fall into her golden hair.

I would go to rehearsals sometimes, study the way she cradled her guitar. Her voice breathy and confident, the rip in the pocket of her leather jacket.

Her bandmates called her "Kat."

I called her Mommy.

She wore combat boots in ninety degrees to prove a point. Her lipstick was darker than a bar after closing and I remember when she didn't want to be called by her real name anymore. "Call me Ivy." She listened to Marilyn Manson and hovered over an Edgar Allen Poe book in church, only slightly pretending to read hymns. I think she wanted everyone to know she hated them. Her once blonde hair was dyed black, and I could only faintly see the little girl I had grown up with through the caked makeup. When the preacher would tell everyone to go around and shake hands with their neighbor, she would stare out from underneath her bangs as if to dare people to say hello to her. I knew it was all an act but I pretended to be afraid of her anyway.

He was sitting outside the cafe smoking a cigarette like it was his last. I never knew someone could look so good in flip flops. He was on television and I loved his work.

He would never date someone like me.

He dated women who walked red carpets and went to Ivy League schools.

Women who were products of two parent households.

Women who got their hair done and were respected in the industry.

Not women who struggle, not me.

I settled for a second glance before I walked away.

We read each other's screenplays, and talked of all the 'one days' people in their 20's talk about. Neither one of us wanted children.

We sat across from one another in intensive workshops, and would gossip about the others after class.

I loved how her hair curled and how she said no to booze, like me.

Before we knew each other we both consumed substances like we had already been forgotten. One night we were in my beautiful two story apartment with the wishing well and the lions.

"I don't want to *be* famous, I just want to look famous and have lots of money," I told her once.

She laughed her perfect laugh, and I loved how she made me feel accepted for my ridiculousness.

I watched her black cat when she went away, and knew she would be my witchy friend forever.

She trudged gloomily along like a waifed dog begging to be fed. There were others like her around and they were all wearing t-shirts that said, 'It's good to be bad.' As I took her photo, she held her chin down without me having to direct her. At the end of the night she asked me to come back to her place for a drink. We listened to Tom Waits while she made a vegan cheese plate in the kitchen. As we sat on the counter drinking rosé she told me that being with me felt like a young friendship that she missed having. "Friendships were the best in sixth grade," I said. "To sixth grade!" she giggled. We held up our glasses and smiled. I fell asleep on her couch watching Now and Then. She covered me up with a blanket and nuzzled her nose with my nose before she blew out the candles.

He sat beside me in the truck. The alley was dark.

"You make me doubt everything," he said.

"We could have done this a long time ago. But we didn't."
His eyes burned into mine for a moment. He thought she was
perfect but I thought she was using him.

Our history was too much and it would never happen.

"I wrote a poem about you," I said "I'll give it to you when
we're old and grey and we'll have a laugh."

He made me promise I wouldn't lose it between then and
grey.

I touched his cheek and said goodbye. When I put my hand
on the door, he asked me not to go.

He made me crab cakes with remoulade.

It was my favorite dish at the time.

He was a beast in the kitchen.

It was what he was meant to do.

We went out on the boat just before the sun went down.

It always had meaning.

"Just us," he said.

Beers in hand because that's what we did.

Reckless.

He always took care of me.

I think he was always longing for something he never had.

We listened to Pearl Jam every day.

I think he was disappointed in how my life turned out, but he never really said it.

"You're my longest relationship," he said as we strolled together down his street. I had heard this line many times before.

"Maybe you forgot about me because you're not watching that show anymore," I replied. He laughed and I didn't and we kept walking. The air was still and being with him felt safe, like nothing bad could ever happen. He grabbed my hand. "You know you're stuck with me right?" This time I laughed and he said I was tantalizing. Later we would lie at the bar to strangers about how we knew each other. *I assisted his mother in Egypt.* The clock struck midnight and we celebrated the New Year, together.

We sat at the cafe before he said goodbye. He showed me a photo of him and a ghost.

"It looks so real, doesn't it?"

I nodded, as it really did.

Afterwards we walked along the streets.

Arm in arm like it was Manhattan in the sixties.

"You are time and women and joy and California," he told me. "And you are my tender heart that lies outside of my body," I replied.

"I love you like the flowers, madly, deeply," he said.

I kissed his cheek and told him he was the brother I always wanted. He promised to keep me updated on his travels, and with arms outstretched we parted ways.

"Why do you always wear your watch on your right hand?" she asked. "You're right-handed."

Her hair was the color of moose tracks and she loved tie dye as much as I did. "Paul McCartney wears his watch on his right hand," I replied defensively. She laughed and exclaimed "Because he's *left-handed*!"

Late at night we would prank call boys we hated in our school.

We would swim naked in the lake outside her house, and she never cared that my family was dysfunctional and without.

Or that I thought hers was perfect and with.

"Why do you always buy clothes when we go to the mall?" she would ask me.

I didn't tell her that I needed them to hide behind.

When I moved to another town she continued to take me on family vacations. Then once she called me and I confused her with another friend.

I don't remember talking to her anymore after that.

"We can play Full Moon in Paris in the background of the ceremony when we get married."

"We'll pause it when she's introducing her friend to her boyfriend."

"And it'll be themed from our favorite movies."

"I'll be Max from Rushmore."

"I'll wear the white silk pajamas his teacher wore. We'll serve spaghetti in one large bowl."

"Gallon wine jugs will fill the tables."

"We can do it our own way."

"You have to have balls to wear pajamas to your own wedding."

"It'll be somewhere really fancy."

"Just spaghetti."

"We'll be happy."

"We'll be really happy."

He talked about his farming, his work and seeds. How they should be in everyone's houses.

I agreed with him as we walked along the compound outside San Diego. His face was the same, and I recalled the time long ago when we sat on the floor of his dorm room.

He had given me a string of beads that he picked up in Morocco. He told me to pray with them.

We played Dave Matthews and didn't touch each other…our relationship wasn't like that

Years later he told his friends "She thinks we're getting married."

We kept walking, and I tried not to be disappointed by him. He was just a nomad living his purpose.

Living his life.

But it is true, sometimes.

Sometimes, people mean more to you

than you do

to them.

We drove up the coast.

He played the CD I made for him.

I stuck my hand out the window and watched the wind make it dance.

It was innocent enough.

I played with the guitar pick he gave me for my birthday.

He said my hands were made for frets

And pens.

We got to the bay.

And watched the silver sunset.

He kissed me like we were the last people on earth.

It wasn't so innocent after that.

And we drove back to the house in silence,

knowing everything had changed. .

He walked into casting.

Tall, with brown eyes and a cheeky grin.

"There's something about him."

I watched as he did something different than the others.

He made suggestions, along with some jokes.

He gave the sweetest smile upon exiting, and after a moment I thought to myself *he's the one*.

The three of us sat at dinner and reminisced on our times of acid and working at bars. "Remember the rock people?" One questioned with excitement. "Goggles!" The other sang, winking and giving me a cheeky grin. I noticed that all of us looked so much better than we had before, healthier and certainly happier. We were mere babies when we lived that life…and it was hard. But as I sat there laughing with them and snacking on hummus and pita bread in the courtyard of the restaurant, a part of me wished we could do it all again…just once.

We played tennis and laughed, while hard kombuchas were sipped in between sets.

We weren't keeping score.

She talked about her dad and how she used to accompany him to markets in New York, when he was young and handsome and the whole world was available to both of them.

I imagined her, tiny and blonde with the same sweet smile. I recognized her Scorpio because I was good at hiding, too. We adored the affluent village where she resided.

"How far we've come!" she yelled as she hit the ball, and I lazily hit it back to her. Isn't it funny when you've known someone forever and yet every day, there's something new to discover about them?

"How do I look?" she asked, as she came out in her regular powder blue nurse's uniform. Red lips and green eyes and perfect silver-blonde hair.

I laughed.

It was the same old thing every night she went to work.

"You look perfect, Grammy."

She laughed and blew me a kiss.

"Au revoir, chérie!" she called in her singsong voice.

I hated when she left and I loved when she returned.

She came into the room we shared together every summer. She whispered timidly "Are you busy?" I put my book down and said of course not. Her face collapsed, and to my surprise she came to me and snuggled up in my arms. "I hate mom," she whispered. I smoothed her sun-kissed hair and stayed quiet as she told me why. I knew there would be a day when she didn't need me anymore.

So I held her tighter, as she cried.

He wore big hats and wrote beautiful songs.

We drove up to Angeles Forest once.

We stared at the horizon in front of us.

"Are you into God?" he asked.

"Yeah, I'm into God. Are you into God?" I replied.

"I'm into God. I could be more into God." He smiled at me. "Some people are too into God..." I assured him.

I put my head on his shoulder, and he started humming a new song he was writing in his head.

Before we got back in the car, he told me I was the real deal.

He took me to the World's End.
Our feet marched in unison.
"We would make good soldiers," he said.
He wore the glasses we bought together in Pisa.
The sun came out just for us.
He told me of a poem a man wrote.
The first line, "I hate seagulls."
I told him I knew a little Norwegian.
He sang songs and lived on his family's farm.
We cuddled at night and he asked if I wanted more.
I said no, this is enough.

We were masked in the grocery store, and we knew we couldn't touch. "If this was a different time, we would have a big hug," he said. "Isn't it amazing that we recognize each other from our eyes?" We stared and exchanged pleasantries.

Then we said goodbye, and wished each other well.

We shared our skittles and took shots together in the back. We found solace in the quiet of the moonlight.

We made each other laugh at bars.

We tiptoed down stairs.

We made promises.

"Hand to God?"

"Do I gotta show him?"

It ended with a lie someone told you.

And you never believed it when I told the truth.

Circling around and around like some French New Wave.

The way we put our hair up.

You never went to class.

I was always afraid to ditch.

You gave me your favorite lipstick.

We chose the boys we wanted around, allowing them to be obsessed with us. The skinny blonde one was a favorite. "He's the Bunnyrabbit of our Antichrist!" you said as we laughed and kissed his cheeks.

I slept in your enormous all white apartment.

Too nice for the likes of our friends who crashed on the floor or in the bathtub.

You stayed up all night painting on the walls and cutting out the labels on all your clothes.

"That kind of stuff doesn't matter."

You were beautiful, so of course that kind of stuff didn't matter.

We ate Flintstones chewable vitamins and talked about how great it was to be skinny.

He told me he would leave his key under the rug outside his flat. I strolled along the sidewalk outside Earl's Court, merrily making my way through Kensington.

Heart pounding.

The newness of London.

The air was salty somehow.

Bitter cold even in May.

I made my way through Redcliffe Gardens.

His beautiful golden key was there for me, just like he said.

I marveled at how trusting strangers could be.

He awoke me gently when he got home from his job at the bank. He looked like a Greek god, and I told him so.

He laughed, and took me to dinner. We mused over mocktails.

He thought it was funny that I didn't drink. When he talked about Belgium, I was disappointed because he made it sound boring.

We went to a place that had egg-shaped toilets.

Then meandered to Soho to listen to jazz.

I wore eyeliner on the tops of my eyelids.

To be mod.

To be something.

"Your eyes are endless," he cooed as he sipped his martini.

I allowed my eyes to wander as they craved closure. Jet lag overcame me and we took a taxi home.

And for a moment we pretended that it was ours.

"There won't be any leftovers," she said as she finished off the broccoli casserole. "No worries," I said, feigning satisfaction. I was still hungry but I figured I could raid the pantry later when she went to sleep. The grey and white tabby cat sat on the floor in front of me, staring into my eyes and flipping her tail back and forth as if to warn me of her sinister nature. "Is her name *really* Kitty Purry?" My friend rolled her eyes and set her plate carefully atop a mountain of dirty dishes. "It's hard for me to stomach as well." She said things differently after she got back from London, but I supposed that was to be expected after two years at an esteemed University. She always had a lot of fanfare whenever she returned from wherever she was…especially from me. The way she dressed was that of a burgeoning aristocrat, and her diction mesmerized me so that it was like walking around with a living, breathing novel.

Mink coats looked good on her. She often had a cigarette in her mouth, and drank nothing but black coffee in glass mugs. Her hair was soft and silver.

Her shoes always matched her handbags.

She played Rummy with the best of them.

On Tuesdays she made lasagna.

Cats from the neighborhood came to her and she fed them as much as she could.

She liked things in the shade of emerald green.

She never remarried when her husband left her.

"He was the best there was, so why would I want anything else?"

She let go of the house she lived in for forty years, and let strangers clean it out.

People stole stuff but she kept her sense of humor, clutching her favorite Mickey Mouse.

She left her body knowing God was taking her home.

We hiked up Holler Mountain.

    She said we were lost.

    She pointed up trails that we had already covered.

    The sun would be down soon, she said.

    So we kept walking, hearing the unnerving howls of coyotes in the distance.

    We found a park ranger.

    He took us to our cabin and said, "This stuff happens all the time."

    Later she and I drank chai tea in bed,
    and promised we would be more careful
    next time.

It was raining in the gardens of Tivoli. The tour guide held his umbrella over me as I took photos with my old Pentax. I wore heels and my mother said to take them off, so I clutched them in my hands as the rain fell. She and I ran around giggling like schoolgirls. Later in the cafe a man came up to us, handsome and confident. He said, "Please, I hope you don't find me rude by saying this, but I was wondering if I could possibly have your phone number. I'm terribly sorry, I'm not trying to interrupt." My mother smiled and I knew she approved of him simply for his thick Irish accent. He and I met several times in England and Los Angeles, and we probably should have gotten married but we didn't.

She was fearless.

She was sure to bludgeon more Ming dynasty priceless china shops with her reckless hooves.

She never knew her father.

Once with a cigarette in her mouth she said that she pissed someone off in a past life.

That now there was no one around to take her sorrows or loneliness

away from her.

She wanted hell instead of heaven. "It's more real," she said.

Once I sat in the backseat of her car on a dirt road close to school with another friend of ours. The girl and I huddled together smoking the weed someone gave me from the west coast. I saw her looking at us through the rearview mirror.

She said she didn't want to be a fucking soccer mom.

My face flushed vermillion and I put the joint out with my fingers. She changed the subject, said she needed to find resolution through her paintings.

She was my hotel California.

An enigma.

She cradled me and yet-

I never really knew her.

There was always a salad made at her house.

She volunteered her time to people in need and stayed true to her word.

Her laugh was better than anyone else's laugh.

She loved figurines of little dogs and working in the garden on the weekends. She ran a radio station for thirty years.

She left her husband when he got violent. And when her next boyfriend got violent, she left him too.

She would rock me back and forth in her chair.

I would watch as her bare feet grazed the carpet beneath her. Her toenails were often painted a pretty color,

a mauve or a pink.

She was everything I could have ever needed in a mother. Perhaps a slightly older version.

She put on Shirley Temple movies for my cousin and I. She wore a lot of red and crocheted doll houses.

So many people loved her, and I wonder if she ever knew how good she was in the world.

He said that he was happy I joined him at his father's birthday.

The whole time I felt proud to be by his side.

I enjoyed meeting the people who loved him so dearly.

"He's the *best,*" his father's friend told me about my date. I smiled and said that I knew that.

Afterwards we walked hand in hand down the middle of the street. We said things to each other we had never said before.

On the way home we gestured as we talked about serious things. As we pulled up to his house, I nudged the universe.

Let him be the one.

As I chewed the cracker in my mouth I said to her "I just tasted my grandmother's house."

"What in the world do you mean?" she asked me, wide-eyed.

"Do you ever have those moments where you taste or smell something, and you can't put your finger on it really but there's a memory there. Your subconscious, perhaps."

"I think maybe we should get a duplex. Separate apartments next to each other," she told me. I put my arm around her.

"We'll have grand parties and I'll dress you for your dates." I imagined at the very least when we were older,

we'd have houses

right next to each other.

He ran the radio, decoded air space in B52's.

I never really understood what it meant when he told me what he did there, and all over the world.

He taught me about music.

We would cover R.E.M. songs in my room after school. He threw away toys he thought I didn't need anymore and congratulated me on my exceptional literary skills.

His ties were always perfect.

He said to me once,

"You're the apple of my eye."

and I never

forgot it.

He spoke of sovereignty of the mind.
    He held on to his mystery and sense of self.
    Like a castle waiting to be galavanted in.
    Waiting to be adored.
    Waiting to be found.
    I knew that he would be loved
    again and again.
    I knew as his lips spoke passion and truth,
    that they would touch other lips that were different
    than mine.
    That he would wander and write and make a soundscape
of realism. Like it was his own backyard.
    All in the world.
    All in time.
    All in a moment.
    And as he spoke of lizards and wolves,
    and how they sacrificed themselves in the desert to feed
others.
    His lips spoke passion.
    And I knew
    that they would eventually touch someone else's
    that were different
    than mine.

She played Dory Previn on the record player.

Ancient tongues sang in a way that made her feel like she was home.

I watched as she fixed her turban and talked about California…how she wanted to accompany me there someday.

When she was better.

I knew that the chaos would stick to her-

That the sickness would stick to her.

"This town breeds possessiveness and it never wants anyone to be happy," she said as she pet her standard poodle.

I agreed with her, but said sometimes people get it right.

And I cried, because she was so beautiful

and I never saw her as anything

other than that.

She got out a box at dinner. She didn't order food.

"They have fries," I said, knowing she didn't eat vegetables.

"I need a job," she said.

"People have jobs," I replied.

And we laughed.

As we sipped our wine, she told me of her desperations.

The days were long gone when I tried to help her.

Because for so many years, I tried and I knew her sanity was out of reach.

So I listened.

And her beautiful blue eyes welled with tears.

The same eyes that I saw wear glasses at night after taking out contacts, wearing too much eyeliner but still looking pretty.

She reached for my hand

and I stared at the constellation tattoo on her arm.

As I held her hand in mine,

I hoped she would make it out of this tumultuous time alive.